NEW YEAR'S DAY 1950...

4

SUNDAY, January 1st 1950, was the beginning of a new decade for the world and a new era for The Broons and Oor Wullie, which would see them scale new heights of popularity in some classic strips.

The New Year was greeted enthusiastically in a country which was still recovering from World War II, with rationing still in force.

The year also started well for Hibernian who were top of the Scottish League with 27 points, four more than nearest rivals Hearts and Rangers.

Radio listeners were promised laughs, quizzes, music and drama over the next few days in shows like 'Ray's A Laugh', 'Top Of The Form', 'Down Your Way', 'Henry Hall's Guest Night', 'Mrs Dale's Diary' and 'Dick Barton — Special Agent', while cinemagoers could see Errol Flynn in 'The New Adventures of Don Juan', Danny Kaye in 'A Song Is Born', Cary Grant in 'Night And Day' and 'Talk Of The Town' and Abbott and Costello with Bela Lugosi in 'Meet The Ghosts'.

Other news included the creations of part-time jobs in nationalised industries, the banning of food parcels from Eire, a sighting of the ghostly 'Black Lady of the Orkneys' and the promise of 'More and Better Ice Cream' to meet Scotland's 'ever-rising demand'.

Illegal Nylons Pouring Into Britain

The Sunday Post, January 8, 1950.

SMALLPOX: 200 HOSPITALS SEALED OFF

SUNDAY, APRIL 2, 1950.

Mass Vaccination May Be Started In Glasgow

SUNDAY, JULY 9, 1950.

Rampant Rangers Had A Shadow East Fife In All But Tatters

The Sunday Post, April 23, 1950.

RANGERS 3, EAST FIFE 0. (Half-time—1-0.)

AMERICANS' GRIM RETREAT AS PANZERS DRIVE ON

U.S. GUNS AND TANKS POUR IN

LONG WAR EXPECTED IN KOREA

SUNDAY, JULY 23, 1950.

NO SWIFT VICTORY, AMERICA WARNED

July — The Korean War was to be headline news for a long time to come.

50

Hundreds Wait In Rain For News Of Princess

Crowds gather outside Clarence House to wait for news of Princess Elizabeth who is expecting her second child, Princess Anne, who was born two days later.

SUNDAY, DECEMBER 31, 1950.

The Stone—Scotland Yard Men Coming North

ARREST RUMOURS DENIED

POLICE, all over Britain were working over-time last night, as the search for the Stone of Destiny became more intense. Leading police officials (normally off dut

Sir Harry Lauder, the Scottish entertainer who became known to millions around the world dies on the 26th of February 1950, aged 79.

THE BROONS AND OOR WULLIE – 1950

The Sunday Post 26th March 1950

THE BROONS AND OOR WULLIE – 1950

The Sunday Post 9th April 1950

THE BROONS AND OOR WULLIE – 1950

THE BROONS AND OOR WULLIE – 1950

THE BROONS AND OOR WULLIE – 1950

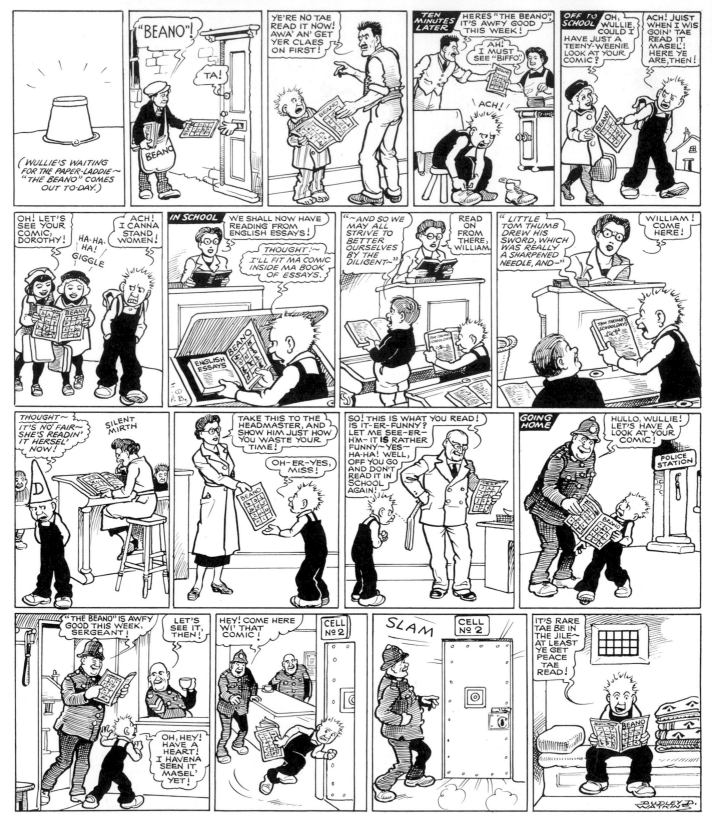

The Sunday Post 3rd December 1950

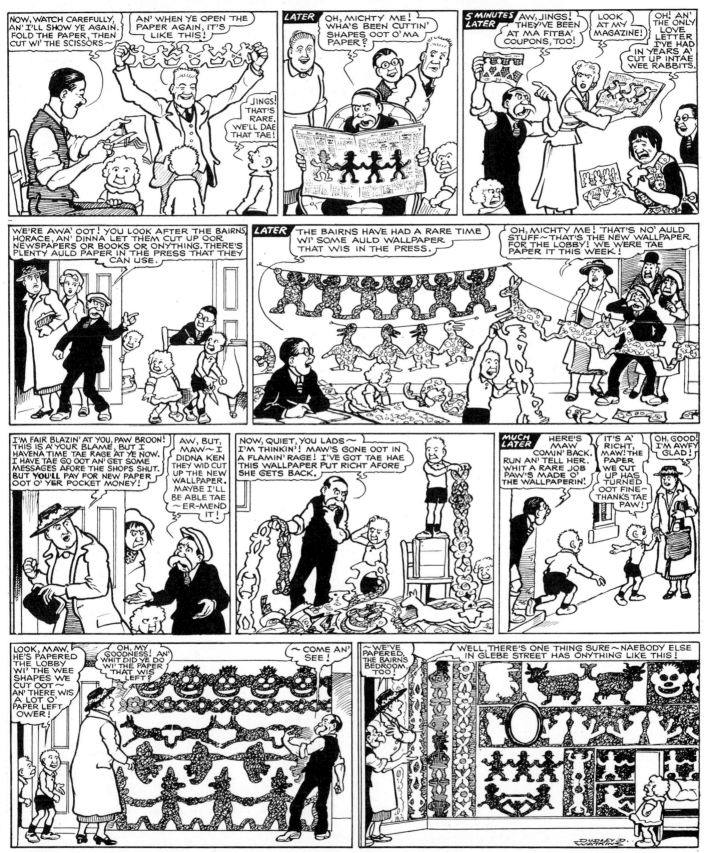

1951

COALMEN PUT GUARDS ON LORRIES AND YARDS
The Sunday Post, January 21, 1951.

Amazing Dodges To Get Coal
BY A SPECIAL CORRESPONDENT

SUNDAY, JULY 8, 1951. RADIO—Page 4.
FLAMES SHOOT 400 FEET HIGH ON SCOTS HILLSIDE

FLYING PETROL TANKER CRASHES: 11 KILLED
SCUERS were driven back

SUNDAY, JULY 1, 1951.
SEARCH FOR RIFLES, AMMO. AND HIDDEN RADIO

PERSIANS RAID OIL H.Q. —SEIZE DOCUMENTS

SUNDAY, SEPTEMBER 23, 1951. RADIO—Page 4.
THE COMMONWEALTH PRAYS FOR HIS MAJESTY THIS MORNING

PALACE PREPARES FOR OPERATION
Doctors Stay All Night Near The King

The Sunday Post, July 22, 1951.
Pies, Bridies, Sausages, Even Haggis, Are All Going Up

HARKNESS AT THE FIN

THE TOAST IS— JOHN M'PHAIL
CELTIC 1, MOTHERWELL 0. (H.-T—1-0).
corer— M'Phail (12 min.).
The Sunday Post, April 22, 1951.

AT THE GENERAL
E AS A NEWSPAPER SUNDAY, APRIL 22, 1951.
CUP-FINAL TRAIN CRASH: 3 KILLED, 70 HURT
WAS the communicati

"The Festival of Britain" had a royal opening on May 4th and was intended as a demonstration of Britain's achievements, way of life and contribution to the world. The 290 foot high Skylon towers above the Festival Dome, which may have inspired the Millennium Dome.

THE BROONS AND OOR WULLIE – 1951

THE BROONS AND OOR WULLIE – 1951

The Sunday Post 11th November 1951

Adapted from the title page of The Broons Book 1955

1952

VERDICT Jack Harkness

MOTHERWELL'S MAGIC MIXTURE DID IT

The Sunday Post, April 20, 1952 13

Februray 17, 1952.

All Day TV Orders Flooded In

FEBRUARY 17, 1952.

AN OLD LADY BRINGS SNOWDROPS FOR THE KING

100,000 IN REMARKABLE PILGRIMAGE TO WINDSOR

OUTSIDE St George's Chapel Wind—

The Sunday Post, May 4, 1952.

CHEERING THOUSANDS GREET THE COMET

'Britain's 'Comet', the first jet air liner service makes its first commercial flight.'

The Sunday Post, June 15, 1952.

Edinburgh Is Agog For The Queen's Visit

SUNDAY, JULY 20, 1952.

Biggest Holiday Crowds For Years

its biggest holiday rush for years yesterday.

'Queen Elizabeth arrives at London airport on February 7th, after an all night flight from Africa, following the death of her father, King George, the previous day.'

The Sunday Post, October 19, 1952.

BEST SAUSAGES SINCE THE WAR

NOVEMBER, 30, 1952.   Radio and

COLDEST NOVEMBER DAY FOR 30 YEARS

FOG AND ICE CAUSE HAVOC IN SCOTLAND

THE BROONS AND OOR WULLIE – 1952

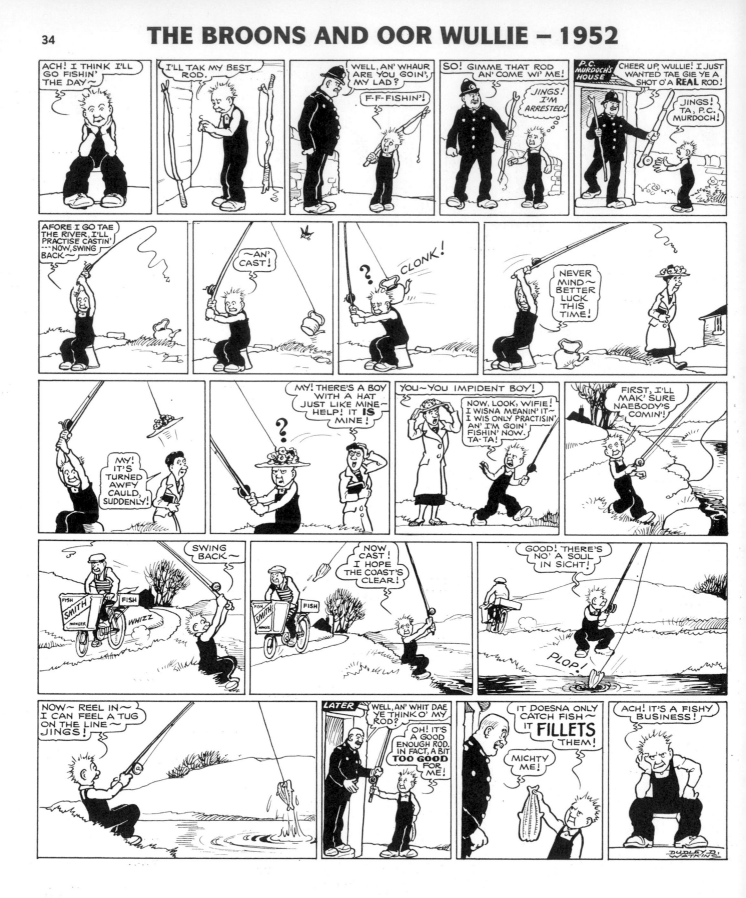

The Sunday Post 24th February 1952

THE BROONS AND OOR WULLIE – 1952

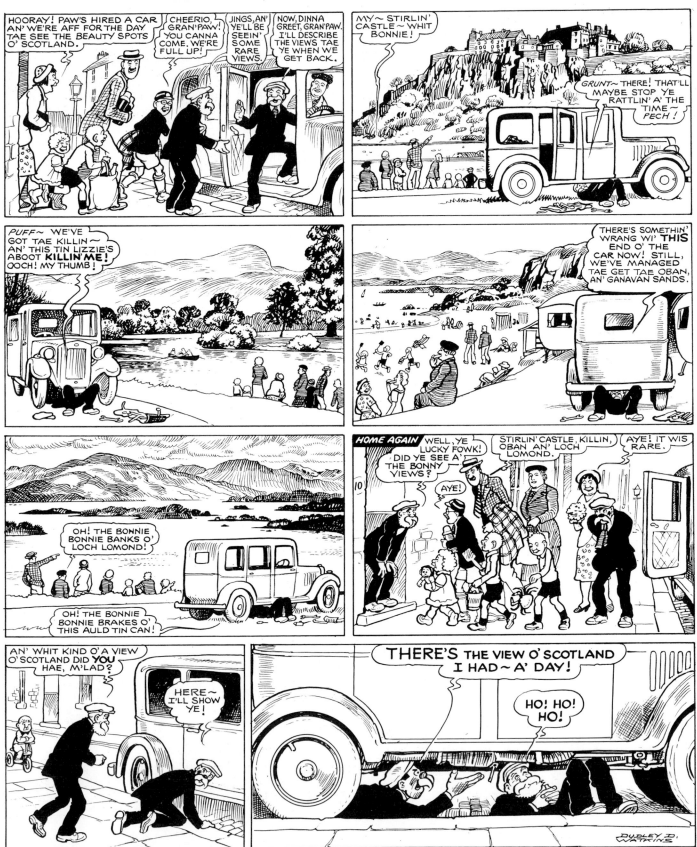

THE BROONS AND OOR WULLIE – 1952

The Sunday Post 18th May 1952

THE BROONS AND OOR WULLIE – 1952

The Sunday Post 15th June 1952

OOR WULLIE

Wullie's Ma kens what to do—
A leather patch'll no' wear through!

Adapted from the title page of The Oor Wullie Book 1956

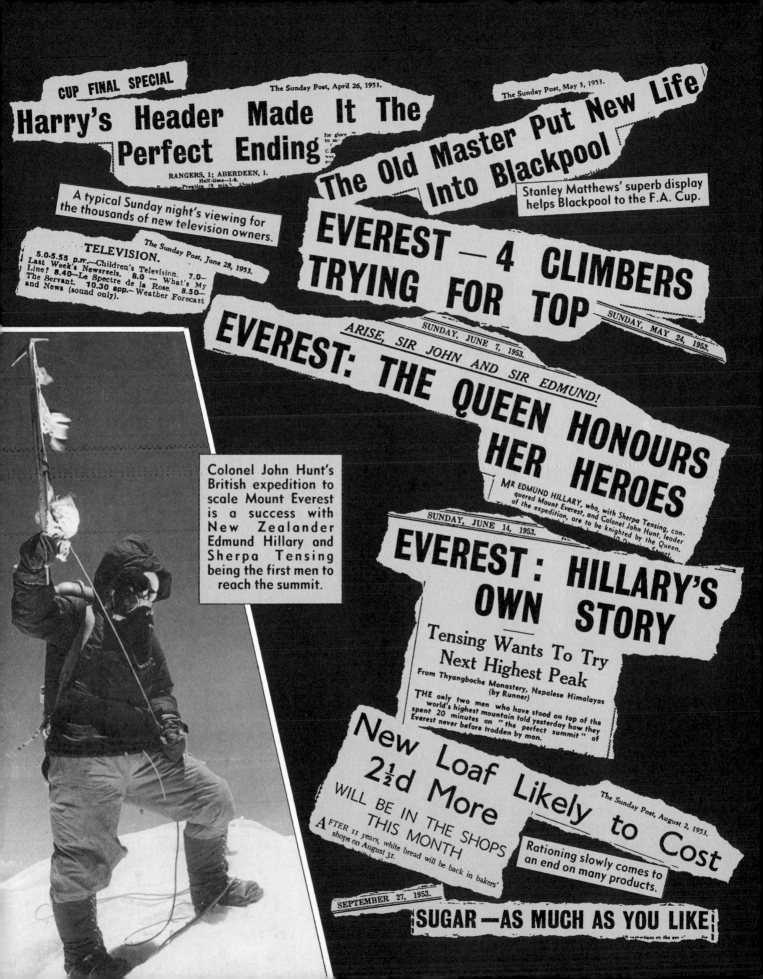

CUP FINAL SPECIAL

The Sunday Post, April 26, 1953.

Harry's Header Made It The Perfect Ending

for glory

RANGERS, 1; ABERDEEN, 1.
Half-time—1-0.

The Sunday Post, May 3, 1953.

The Old Master Put New Life Into Blackpool

Stanley Matthews' superb display helps Blackpool to the F.A. Cup.

A typical Sunday night's viewing for the thousands of new television owners.

The Sunday Post, June 28, 1953.

TELEVISION.
5.0-5.55 p.m.—Children's Television. 7.0—Last Week's Newsreels. 8.0 — What's My Line? 8.40—Le Spectre de la Rose. 8.50—The Servant. 10.30 app.— Weather Forecast and News (sound only).

EVEREST — 4 CLIMBERS TRYING FOR TOP

SUNDAY, MAY 24, 1953.

SUNDAY, JUNE 7, 1953.

ARISE, SIR JOHN AND SIR EDMUND!

EVEREST: THE QUEEN HONOURS HER HEROES

MR EDMUND HILLARY, who, with Sherpa Tensing, conquered Mount Everest, and Colonel John Hunt, leader of the expedition, are to be knighted by the Queen.

Colonel John Hunt's British expedition to scale Mount Everest is a success with New Zealander Edmund Hillary and Sherpa Tensing being the first men to reach the summit.

SUNDAY, JUNE 14, 1953.

EVEREST: HILLARY'S OWN STORY

Tensing Wants To Try Next Highest Peak

From Thyangboche Monastery, Nepalese Himalayas (by Runner)

THE only two men who have stood on top of the world's highest mountain told yesterday how they spent 20 minutes on "the perfect summit" of Everest never before trodden by man.

New Loaf Likely to Cost 2½d More

WILL BE IN THE SHOPS THIS MONTH

AFTER 11 years, white bread will be back in bakers' shops on August 31.

The Sunday Post, August 2, 1953.

Rationing slowly comes to an end on many products.

SEPTEMBER 27, 1953.

SUGAR —AS MUCH AS YOU LIKE

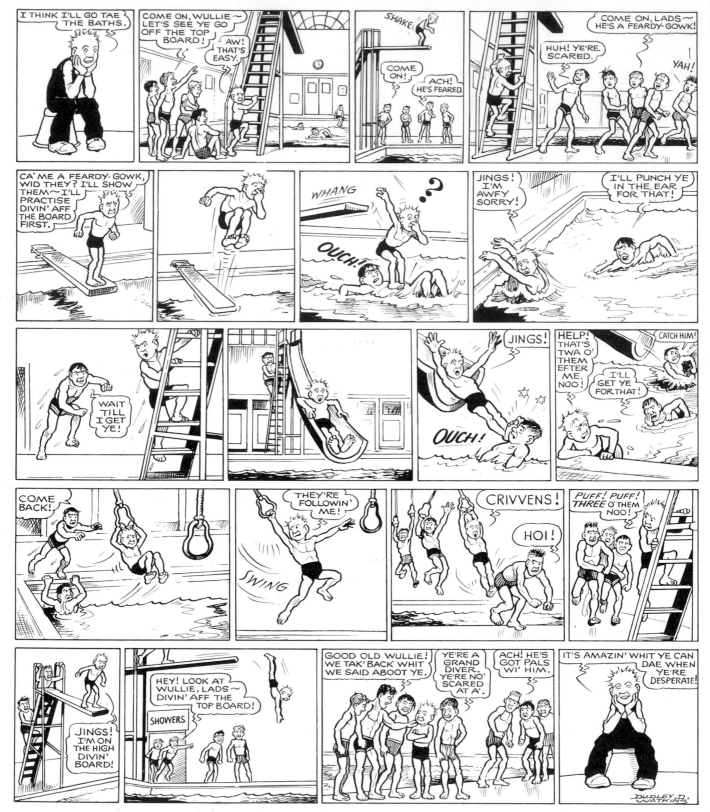

The Sunday Post 26th July 1953

THE BROONS AND OOR WULLIE – 1953

THE BROONS AND OOR WULLIE – 1953

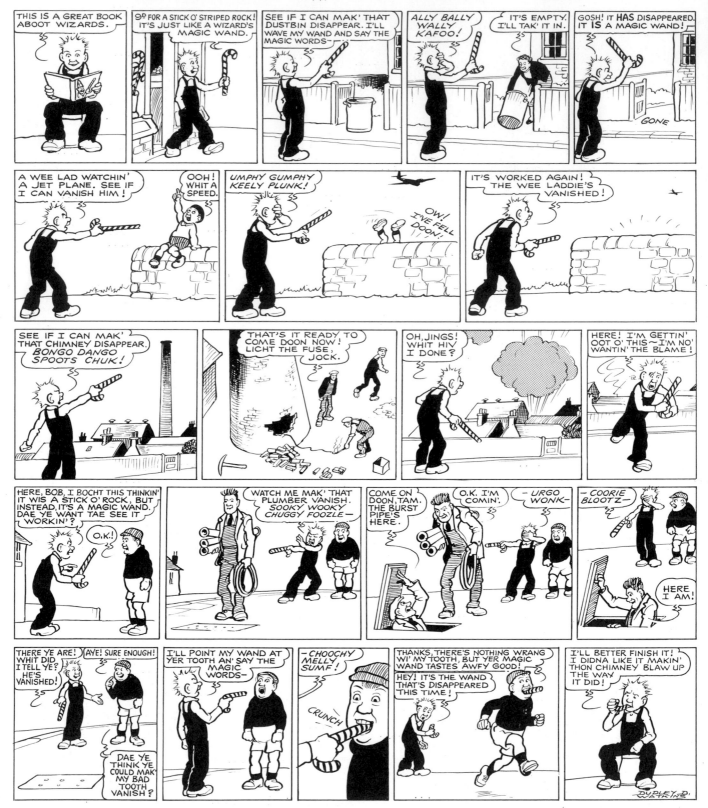

1954

Sunday Post, January 17, 1954.
AFTERMATH OF SCOTLAND'S 97 m.p.h. GALE

THE WIND WHIPPED AWAY HUTS, ROOFS, COAL—AND SAUSAGES

A housewife from Glasgow gets a shock when the wind blows a long string of sausages round her neck.

The Sunday Post, May 9, 1954.

BUTTER AND MARG OFF THE RATION TODAY

BUTTER, cheese, margarine and cooking fats are off the ration from today—the first time in 14 years.

The Sunday Post, September 26, 1954.

Glasgow Mothers Try To End A "Vampire" Panic

Rumours of a monster prowling in the Southern Necropolis in Glasgow cause a scare amongst local children.

SUNDAY, JULY 4, 1954.
RUMP STEAK AT 7s 6d A LB. IN LONDON

THE BATTLE OF THE BEEF PRICES IS ON

Eating

BEEF will cost anything from 8d to 1s 6d ... more tomorrow. This ... Scottish but ...

PUBLISHED EVERY SUNDAY
SUNDAY, MAY 23, 1954.
SCOTLAND WILL BE IN THE LEAD

GREAT NEW DRIVE TO CLEAR THE SLUMS

The Sunday Post, June 13, 1954.

APPEAL TO THE BROONS

WE can't get fixed up for our holidays and we were wondering if the Broons could let us have their but and ben for the Glasgow Fair. —
Four Factory Girls, Glasgow.

● Hen, Joe, Paw and Granpaw say — *"Send your photies an' we'll think it over!"* But Horace, the Twins, and the Bairn say — *"More dames? Nuts! We've enuff already."* — Editor.

The Sunday Post, December 12, 1954.

WE'LL EAT WOOD IN 2000 A.D.!

THE Royal Society of Arts, in the current journal, ...

The Royal Society of Arts journal publishes a summary of forecasts of life at the turn of the millenium submitted by readers. Predictions include London being covered by a single plastic dome, sugar being made from wood (with any non food uses for wood prohibited in the U.S.A.), compulsory vegetarianism and advertisements being projected into the night sky, with space sold according to the position of the stars.

Roger Bannister breaks the four minute mile barrier at the Iffley Road track in Oxford on the sixth of May.

"TEDDY BOYS" INVADE CLYDE COAST TOWNS

The Sunday Post, May 23, 1954.

THE BROONS AND OOR WULLIE – 1954

The Sunday Post 11th April 1954

The Sunday Post 6th June 1954

The Sunday Post 11th July 1954

The Sunday Post 24th October 1954

The Sunday Post 5th December 1954

Adapted from the title page of *The Broons Book 1953*

1955

SUNDAY, JANUARY 23, 1955.

American Aircraft Carriers Are On The Way To Formosa

IKE TO WARN CHINA: "WE FIGHT IF—"

the Sunday Post, March 6, 1955.

TEA—MORE PRICE CUTS

But Some Qualities Will Be Lower

March 6, 1955.

FLYING SAUCER OVER BUCKIE!

Three Men And A Woman Say They Saw It

SUNDAY, APRIL 3, 1955.

SIR WINSTON EXPECTED TO RESIGN ON TUESDAY

Campbell Means To Go Faster Yet!

SUNDAY, JULY 24, 1955.

DONALD CAMPBELL, who broke the world water speed record yesterday, hopes to go faster still. he announced that—if con his—

April 24, 1955.

CORNER KICK THAT SAVED A DAMP SQUIB FINAL

CELTIC 1. CLYDE 1.

Queen Sells Biscuits—Is Told "Keep The Change"

Memorable Scenes At Royal Sale Of Work

SUNDAY, AUGUST 21, 1955.

the Sunday Post, May 1, 1955.

100,000 HEAR BILLY GRAHAM AT HAMPDEN

a million relay centres in England,

28 years old Ruth Ellis is the last woman to be executed in Britain.

Billy Graham's six week All-Scotland-Crusade draws huge crowds.

The Sunday Post, July 10, 1955.

10,000 MORE SIGN RUTH ELLIS PETITION

The Sunday Post, December 25, 1955.

No Dumpling On Muckle Flugga

Muckle Flugga, Britain's most northerly lighthouse, is made inaccessible by rough sea conditions, with the lightkeepers' families unable to send any Christmas presents or food.

THE BROONS AND OOR WULLIE – 1955

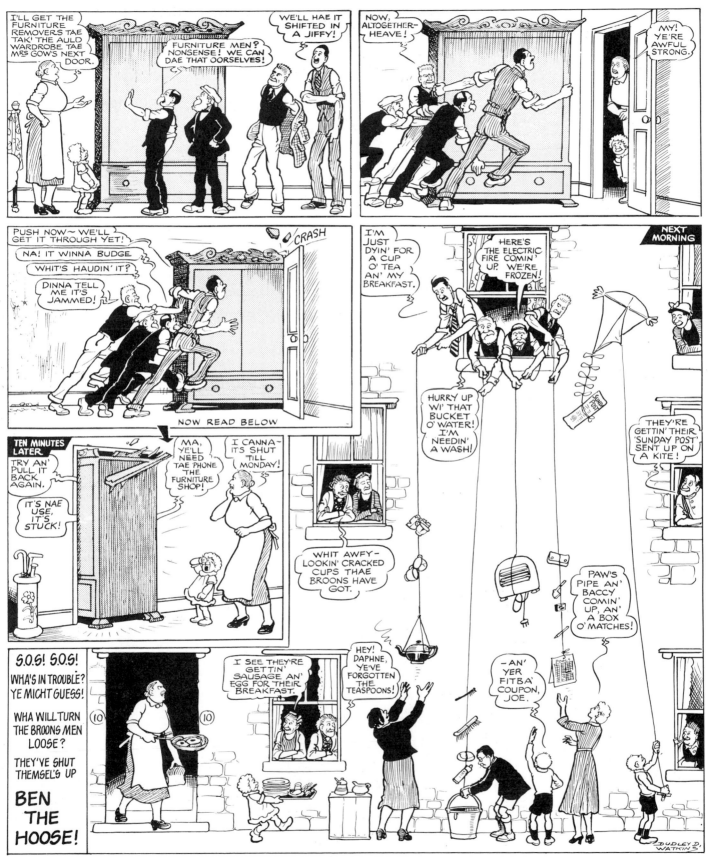

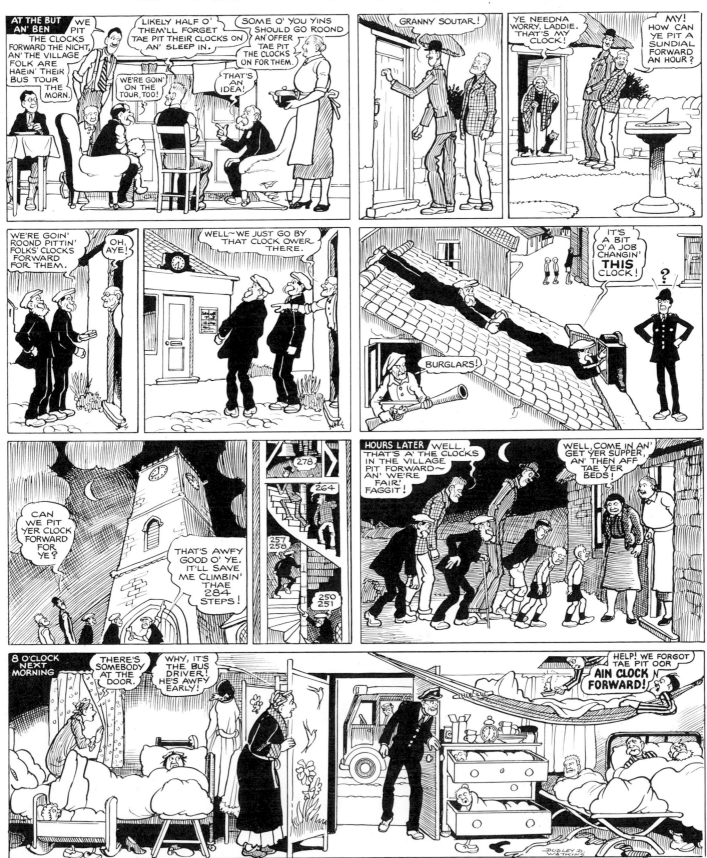

The Sunday Post 17th April 1955

THE BROONS AND OOR WULLIE – 1955

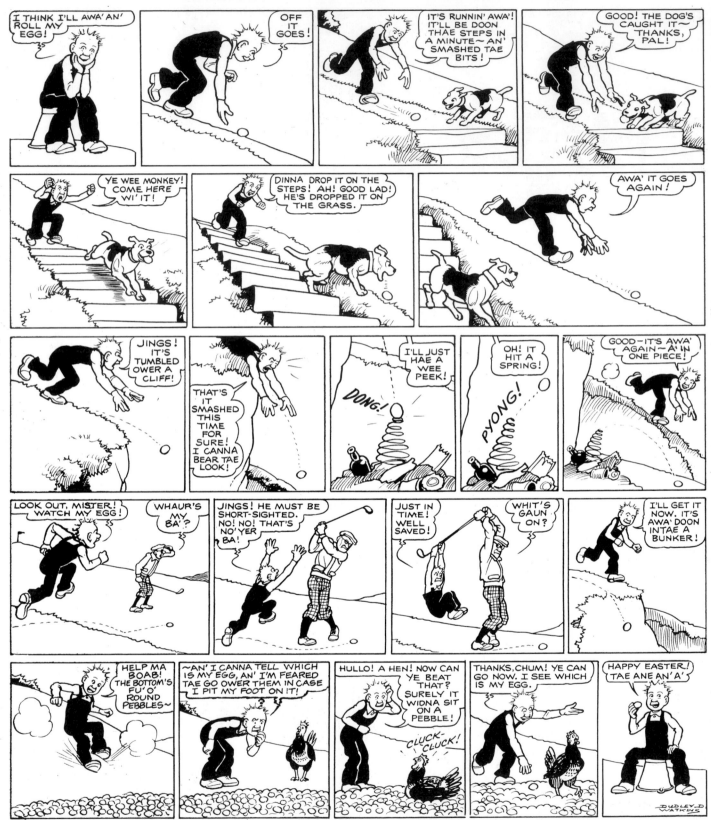

THE BROONS AND OOR WULLIE – 1955

THE BROONS AND OOR WULLIE – 1955

1956

SUNDAY, FEBRUARY 12, 1956

Burgess And Maclean Tell Their Story

After Dramatic Reappearance In Moscow

The Sunday Post, April 22, 1956.

Hap-Hap-Happy Hearts

THANKS TO A CRACKSHOT CAMERON HIGHLANDER

HEARTS, 3; CELTIC, 1.
(Half-time: Hearts, 1; Celtic, 0).

Edinburgh Goes Daft!

"We Shall Meet Force With Force." Shouts Nasser

SUNDAY, JULY 29, 1956.

SUEZ: WEST'S VITAL TALKS TODAY

ARMY STOPS DEMOB OF REGULARS

SUEZ: WEEK-END MOVES

SUNDAY, AUGUST 5, 1956.

SUEZ CRISIS — FLEET OF SHIPS NOW AT PORTSMOUTH

The Sunday Post, September 2, 1956.

"Heartbreak Hotel" is released in January, reaching No. 2 in the British Charts. Within a year, Elvis Presley wins six gold discs, makes his movie debut in "Love Me Tender" and becomes a worldwide phenomenon.

EGYPT TELLS BRITONS: "GET OUT!"

13,000

SUNDAY, NOVEMBER 25, 1956.

Mass Expulsion Unprecedented
EGYPT is to expel all British and French subjects within seven to ten days.

SUNDAY, DECEMBER 9, 1956.

Dog (In Space Suit) Goes Up 70 Miles!

A DOG

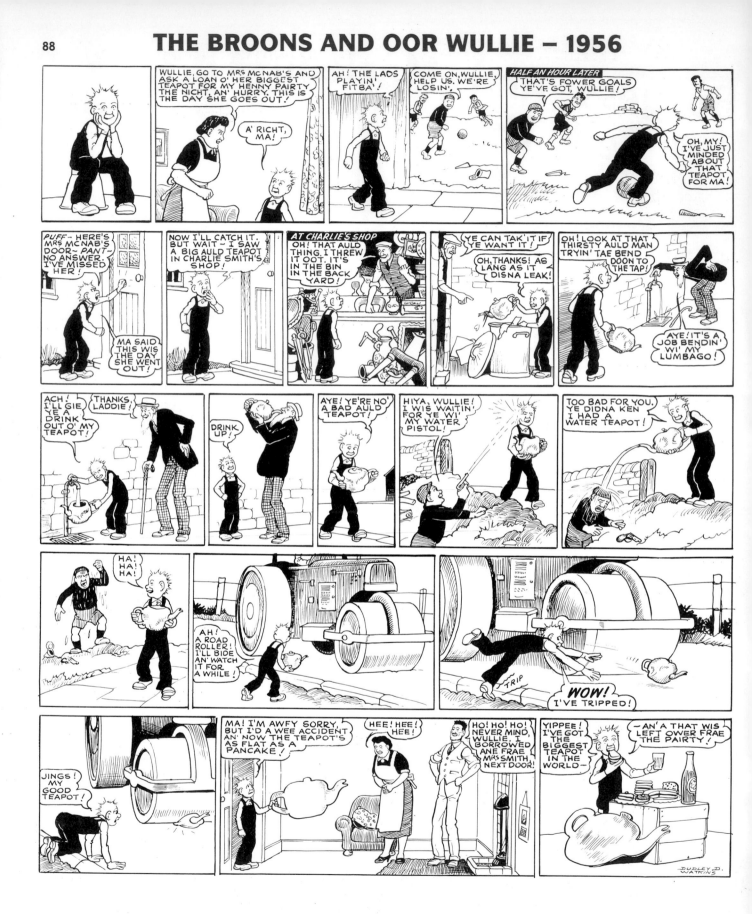

The Sunday Post 12th February 1956

The Sunday Post 11th March 1956

THE BROONS AND OOR WULLIE – 1956

The Sunday Post 19th August 1956

THE BROONS AND OOR WULLIE – 1956

The Sunday Post 21st October 1956

THE BROONS AND OOR WULLIE – 1956

Adapted from the title page of *The Oor Wullie Book 1952*

1957

Laika, 'the Space Dog', was sent into space on the second Russian satellite to test the safety of space travel.

SUNDAY, FEBRUARY 10, 1957.

Glasgow Man Bitten By A Lion

A man is bitten by a lion, just off Argyle Street in Glasgow. The lion, in Wilson's Zoo, attacked after being offered a caramel.

The Sunday Post, June 16, 1957.

Look— There's A Dog Smoking A Pipe

TRIUMPH OF THE "OLD HEADS"

The Sunday Post, April 21, 1957. 27

Falkirk Trio The Cup Final Heroes

KILMARNOCK 1, FALKIRK 1
Half-Time, 1-1.

Longer And Stronger Runways—A New Control Tower

The Sunday Post, August 25, 195

PRESTWICK GETS READY FOR JET AGE

The Sunday Post, March 3, 1957.

ROCK 'N' ROLL BUDGIE

Tony, a wonder

The Sunday Post, October 6, 1957.

Millions Hear Signals From Russia's Space Satellite

FIRST STAGE IN FLIGHT TO THE MOON"

SUNDAY, SEPTEMBER 1, 1957.

S.T.V.'S FIRST NIGHT

Independent television begins broadcasting in Scotland.

SUNDAY, NOVEMBER 10, 1957.

As Sputnik No. 1 Spirals Down Towards Earth

A NEW OBJECT IN THE SKY: IS IT BID TO HIT MOON?

SUNDAY, NOVEMBER 10,

Edinburgh Women Get "Flying Saucer" Scare

A LOAD of women day

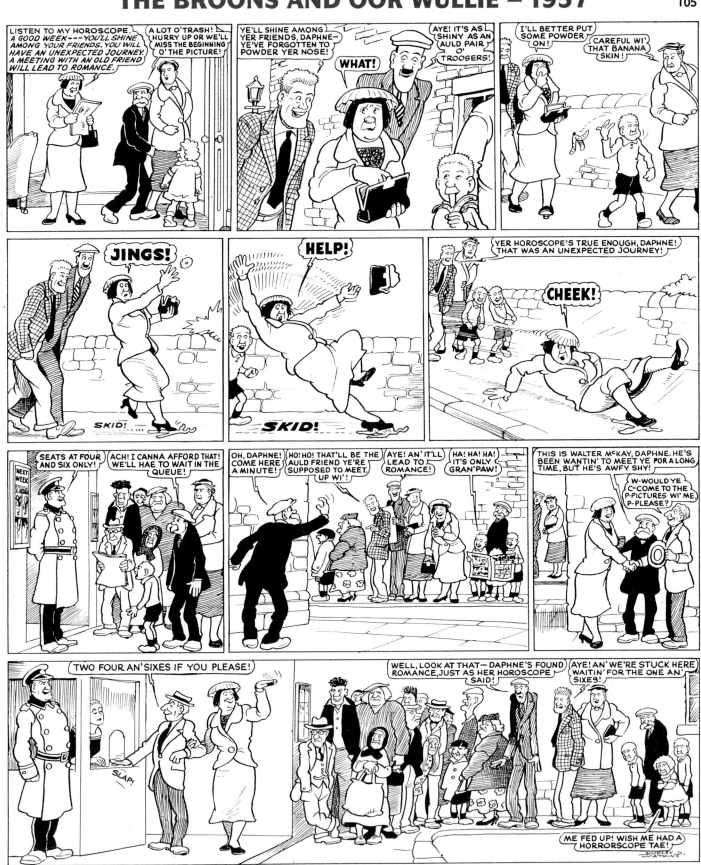

THE BROONS AND OOR WULLIE – 1957

The Sunday Post 3rd March 1957

The Sunday Post 28th April 1957

THE BROONS AND OOR WULLIE – 1957

THE BROONS AND OOR WULLIE – 1957

The Sunday Post 29th December 1957

1958

We'll Have Power Of Veto On Use Of Missiles

SUNDAY, FEBRUARY 23, 1958.

BRITAIN SIGNS ROCKET BASES PACT

The Sunday Post, April 27, 1958.

Field Marshal Robertson

PLUCKY HIBS —BUT CLYDE DESERVE CUP

CLYDE 1. HIBS 0.

SUNDAY, FEBRUARY 2, 1958.

The Sunday Post, April 27, 1958.

More Pears, Peaches, And Fruit Cocktail!

Now It's A Race For The Moon!

AMERICA was jubilant last night as her first satellite rocketed round the world at 18,000 miles an hour. ALL THE DISAPPOINTMENT AFTER THE FAILURE TO

The Sunday Post, May 25, 1958.

Dounreay Switches On—Scotland Enters Atom Age

SUNDAY, JULY 20, 1958.

"In This Grave Hour"

KRUSHCHEV CALLS FOR GENEVA TALKS

Macmillan, Eisenhower, De Gaulle, Nehru And U.N. Chief Invited

SUNDAY, JULY 27, 1958.

Queen's Dramatic Message To Empire Games

CHARLES—PRINCE OF WALES!

SUNDAY, AUGUST 17, 1958.

All Set For Take-Off At Dawn Today!

MOON BID THIS MORNING

—SAYS MESSAGE FROM CAPE CANAVERAL

Pele's goals help Brazil to a 5-2 victory against Sweden in the World Cup final.

Remarkable Scenes After Announcement

"I HAVE decided to create my son, Prince Charles, Prince of Wales."

The Sunday Post, November 9, 1958.

Moon Bid Fails—Now It's Up To U.S. Army

The Sunday Post 8th June 1958

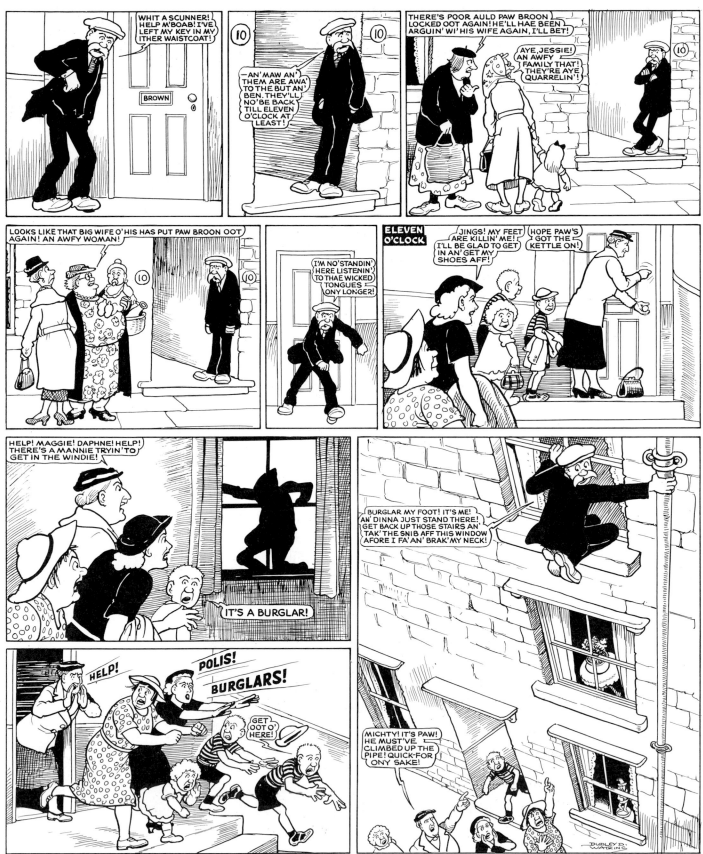

The Sunday Post 20th July 1958

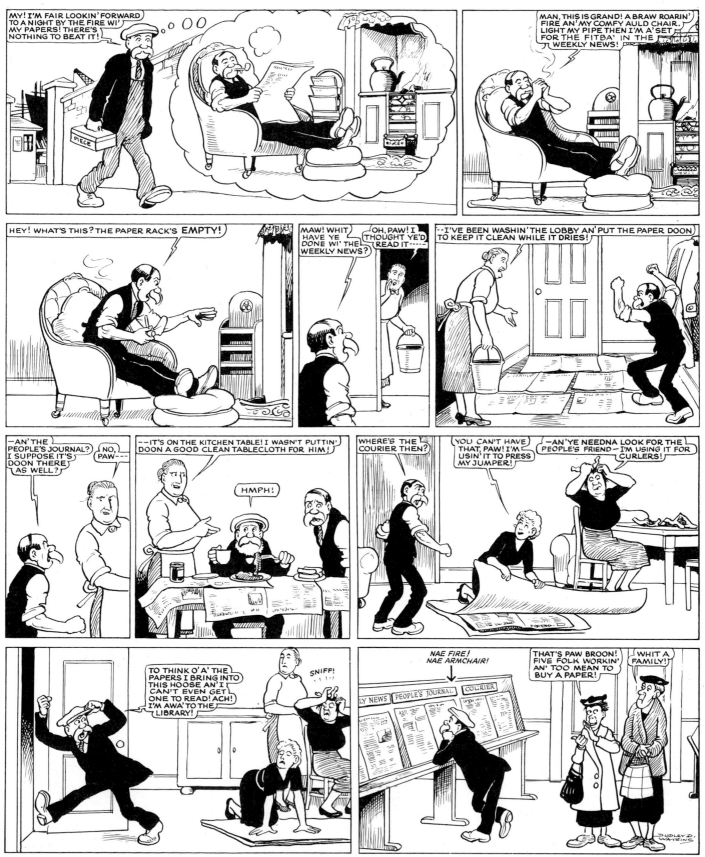

THE BROONS AND OOR WULLIE – 1958

THE BROONS

Adapted from the title page of The Broons Book 1957

1959

The Sunday Post, April 26, 1959.

DONS COULDN'T MATCH SAINTS' WILL-TO-WIN SPIRIT

ST MIRREN 3, ABERDEEN 1.
Mirren—Bryceland

The Sunday Post, February 15, 1959.

No Stiletto Heels Allowed

The Sunday Post, March 29, 1959.

EDINBURGH TO LONDON —BY LAWNMOWER!

The Mini, often perceived as a symbol of the swinging sixties was actually launched in 1959. Its place as a design classic of the twentieth century is assured.

The Sunday Post, May 31, 1959.

The King Of Clocks Is 100 Years Old Today

£25 Stolen From Funnel Of Butcher's Sausage Machine, Then—

The Sunday Post, June 14, 1959.

Injured Thief Breaks Into Chemist's Shop For Bandages

The Sunday Post, March 29, 1959.

Budgie Learns Gaelic!

President Eisenhower flies by Comet from Balmoral to Chequers for talks with Prime Minister Macmillan, concerning Berlin. The dinner included consommé brunoise, grilled fillets of sole, and bacon rolls.

The Sunday Post, November 22, 1959.

Now The Broons Have a Bar— In Glebe Street, Too

MOST folk bump into the Broons only once a week — in the fun section of "The Sunday Post." But in Townhead, Glasgow, they're bumping into them every day. In Glebe Street—yes, Glebe Street—there's a wee pub on the corner run by a Mr Jack Brown.

SUNDAY, AUGUST 30, 1959.

IKE AND MAC GET DOWN TO BUSINESS

Talks— Then Golf On Lawn

SUNDAY, NOVEMBER 22, 1959.

CONDEMNED FOR 20 YEARS

Families In Terror As Tenement Crashes

The Sunday Post 4th January 1959

THE BROONS AND OOR WULLIE – 1959

The Sunday Post 4th October 1959

THE BROONS AND OOR WULLIE – 1959

It's time tae bring the curtain door,
on dugs in space that orbit roon',
on Everest, rationin' and rock 'n' roll,
Fower minute miles, and Pele's goal.
It's farewell tae the Fifties.

Printed and Published in Great Britain by D.C. Thomson & Co., Ltd., 185 Fleet Street, London EC4A 2HS.
© D.C. THOMSON & CO., LTD. 1998.
ISBN 0 85116 678 4